Step-by-Step
50 Perfect Pasta Dishes

Step-by-Step

50 Perfect Pasta Dishes

Maxine Clark

Photography by Edward Allwright

CLB

Colour Library Books

CLB 4247

Colour Library Books Ltd
Godalming Business Centre
Woolsack Way
Godalming
Surrey GU7 1XW
United Kingdom

© Anness Publishing Limited 1994
Boundary Row Studios
1 Boundary Row
London SE1 8HP

Reprinted in 1995

ISBN 1 85833 194 3

Editorial Director: Joanna Lorenz
Series Editor: Lindsay Porter
Assistant Editor: Charles Moxham
Designers: Peter Butler, Peter Laws
Photographer: Edward Allwright
Stylist: Hilary Guy

Printed and bound in Hong Kong

MEASUREMENTS

*Three sets of equivalent measurements have been provided in the recipes here, in the following
order: Metric, Imperial and American. It is essential that units of measurement are not mixed
within each recipe. Where conversions result in awkward numbers, these have been rounded for
convenience, but are accurate enough to produce successful results.*

CONTENTS

INTRODUCTION

Pasta has rapidly become one of today's staple foods, travelling across the world in various forms as far as Asia and South America. Its origins are unclear, but a type of pasta was certainly made in Sicily, the 'grain store' of Rome, in the days of the Roman Empire. It has also existed in China and Japan for many centuries, but in very different forms and shapes.

The enormous popularity of pasta is due to its incredible versatility, and its value for money. Pasta can stretch a few store-cupboard ingredients to make a satisfying meal fit for a king! You can produce sauces with small amounts of meat, mix them with pasta and produce a filling and nutritious dish. Most wheat-flour-and-water (commercial dried) pasta contains more proteins and carbohydrates than potatoes, so when combined with a sauce of vegetables, cheese or meat, it gives a good nutritional balance. It is a fine source of energy too – better than sugar, as it releases energy at a slower prolonged rate, and will give you a lift if you are tired and hungry. Pasta is only fattening if eaten in over-large quantities with too much sauce! Italians fill up on the pasta itself, the sauce being an adornment to enhance the flavour.

Pasta is very easy to make at home if you have patience and a little time to spare. The result is exciting and delicious, even if it is a little soggy to begin with! It's a little like making bread: once you have mastered the technique, you can make one of life's staples. Fresh egg pasta is made *only* with wheat flour, eggs, a little salt and olive oil. Do not be tempted to add water as it will toughen the pasta and make it sticky. The main thing is to enjoy the process and the results *con gusto*.

Pasta Types

When buying dried pasta, choose good-quality well-known brands. Of the 'fresh' pasta sold in sealed packs in supermarkets, the filled or stuffed varieties are worth buying; noodles and ribbon pasta are better bought dried, as these tend to have more bite when cooked. However, if you are lucky enough to live near an Italian delicatessen where pasta is made on the premises, it will usually be of very good quality. Fresh is not necessarily better, but the final choice is yours – the best pasta is home-made, as then you can be sure of the quality of the ingredients used and also of the finished texture.

You will see from this book that the sauces are almost limitless in their variety, as are the pasta shapes themselves. There are no hard-and-fast rules regarding which shape to use with which pasta sauce: it's really a matter of personal preference. However, there are a few guidelines to follow, such as that thin spaghetti suits seafood sauces, thicker spaghetti is good with creamy sauces (as in, for instance, Spaghetti alla Carbonara) and thick tubular pasta, like rigatoni, penne and so on, suits rustic sauces full of bits that will be caught in the pasta itself.

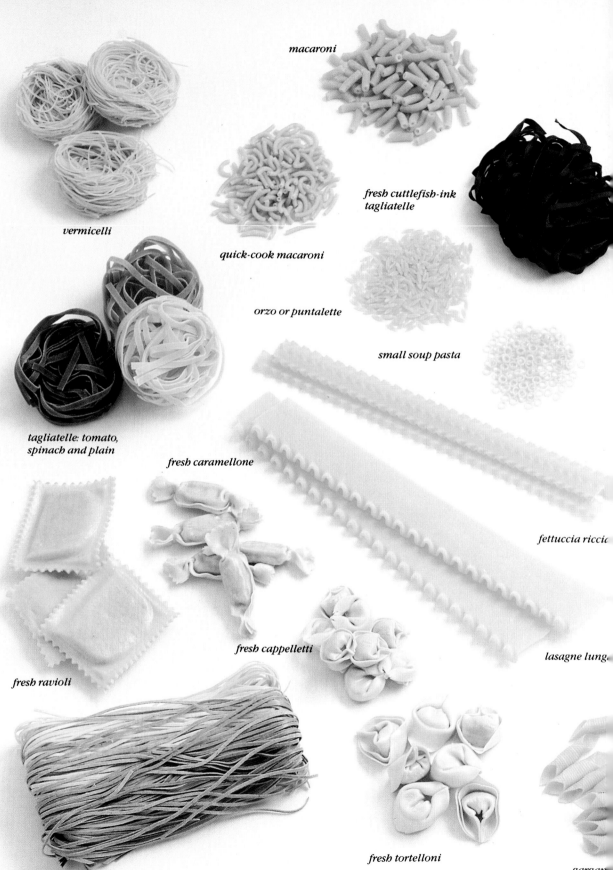

macaroni

vermicelli

quick-cook macaroni

fresh cuttlefish-ink tagliatelle

orzo or puntalette

small soup pasta

tagliatelle: tomato, spinach and plain

fresh caramellone

fettuccia riccia

fresh ravioli

fresh cappelletti

lasagne lung.

fresh tortelloni

gargan.

'paglia e fieno' ('straw and hay' tagliarini)

sh papperdelle

fresh beetroot
tagliatelle

fresh wild-mushroom
tagliatelle

conchigliette rigate
(small soup pasta shells)

spaghetti

spinach spaghetti

wholemeal (wholewheat) spaghetti

pipe rigate

pasta bows (farfalle)

campanelle

cannelloni

spirali

rigatoni

pasta shells (conchiglie)

lasagne

spinach lasagne

wholemeal (wholewheat) shells

orecchite

Herbs and Spices

Both fresh and dried herbs can be used successfully to enhance the flavour of most pasta sauces. Certain herbs have an affinity with particular ingredients, and are added to bring out their flavours or to accentuate them. Tomatoes are the natural sauce ingredient, and their taste can be changed completely by the incorporation of different herbs and spices. Fresh herbs, although expensive in supermarkets, are a must for a sauce like pesto. Dried basil has none of the Mediterranean pungency needed in this wonderfully evocative sauce. The colour of fresh herbs brings a visual charm to sauces, as well as adding a truly fresh flavour. Buy growing herbs in pots and – despite instructions to the contrary on the packaging – try planting them out in the garden in summer or, as I do, in a windowbox. They will grow in a sunny, well-drained spot if cut regularly (but not too much). Stating that they cannot be planted out is a commercial ploy to make you buy more.

Ideally use fresh herbs immediately after cutting, but if you have to keep them for any length of time, most will store well in a jar of water covered with a sealed polythene bag and placed in the refrigerator.

Dried herbs are very useful if they are not too old. Freeze-dried are the best as they retain both colour and flavour. Use half the quantity of dried herbs as you would fresh, for the flavour is more concentrated. Store dried herbs in air-tight containers, in a dark dry cupboard.

Basil
Fresh basil is *the* herb for pasta dishes, and dried basil is a poor substitute. If fresh basil is unavailable, use a spoonful of ready-made pesto sauce instead of the dried herb for a better taste. The flavour is a pungent mixture of cinnamon and anise: it is too difficult to describe, so just find some and use it – the more, the better! Basil is wonderful with tomatoes and in delicate ricotta cheese fillings. It is lost, however, in hearty meaty sauces.

Bay leaves
Bay is often used to enhance the flavour of meat sauces and to give a delicate flavour to béchamel or white sauces.

Dill (dillweed)
A herb with a slightly aniseed flavour which marries well with fish, especially fresh or smoked salmon.

Garlic
Used in moderation, garlic is a marvellous flavour enhancer. However, the longer you cook it, the more mellow the flavour. It is good in most dishes where a strong onion taste is required – meat sauces, anything with tomato, and with pulses and beans. Choose big fat cloves for a fuller, less bitter flavour.

Oregano and marjoram
Oregano and marjoram are the most popular herbs used in Italy, along with basil and sage. They have an affinity with tomatoes and eggs, and make a pretty garnish when in flower. Oregano is a wilder strain and more astringent than marjoram, which has a sweeter flavour.

Parsley (curly and flat-leaf)
Parsley is a very versatile herb and both types of parsley impart a fresh 'green' flavour to almost any dish. The common curly variety is good for chopping and the pretty flat-leafed one is lovely roughly chopped or used as a leafy garnish. A delicious pesto sauce can be made using parsley instead of basil.

Rocket (arugula)
Rocket, with its slightly peppery taste, can be used both as a herb and, more commonly, as a salad ingredient. In this book it is simply stirred into a pasta dish at the end of cooking so that it wilts like spinach, but is still crunchy.

Sage
A classic Italian herb available in many varieties. It has a lovely earthy flavour and is good with meat and some cheeses such as Gorgonzola.

Chillies (dried and fresh)
Use smaller quantities of dried chillies than fresh – they add heat and spiciness to sauces such as arrabbiata. Wear rubber gloves when preparing fresh chillies, or work under running water, and don't rub your eyes as the juice of both dried and fresh chillies can be painful. Green or red chillies can be used – the quantities are variable depending on your taste, but to be on the safe side add less than specified in the recipe: you can always add more.

Nutmeg
The kernel of a nut that also produces mace, nutmeg gives a rich musky flavour to white sauces and is good with cheese.

Saffron
These orange filaments are the stigma of the saffron crocus, one of the world's most expensive spices, but a little goes a long way. Saffron is also available in powdered form. This delicate spice will impart a wonderful aroma and colour to any dish.

dried chillies

bay

saffron

rocket (arugula)

oregano

dill (dillweed)

sage

basil

garlic

fresh chillies

flat-leaf parsley

nutmeg

curly parsley

purple marjoram

Sauces and Pastes

There is an infinite variety of ready-made sauces and pastes available which you can add to your own sauce to make it richer or to deepen the flavour. Some can even be incorporated into pasta dough: for example, you can make mushroom or tomato or even pesto pasta.

Anchovies: salted
Whole anchovies preserved in salt which need to be rinsed and the backbone removed before use. They have a a fresher flavour than canned anchovy fillets in oil. Used in moderation, anchovies add a fishy depth to sauces and soups.

Capers
These are little green flower buds picked before they open and preserved in vinegar or salt. They add a sharp piquancy to rich sauces and are particularly good with tomatoes and cheese.

Carbonara sauce
Although your own version made from the recipe in this book will be much better, ready-made carbonara sauce is a useful standby for a quick meal – add sautéed fresh mushrooms or more bacon to make it go further.

Garlic: chopped
A great time-saver, eliminating the need for peeling and chopping. Use it straight out of the jar.

Mushroom paste
A delicacy available from Italian delicatessens. Add a generous spoonful to freshly cooked pasta with a little cream for a quick sauce, or to pasta dough to make mushroom pasta.

Olive paste
Cuts out all that stoning (pitting) and chopping. Delicious stirred into hot pasta with chopped fresh tomato or added by the spoonful to enrich a tomato or meat sauce.

Pesto
The commercial version of fresh basil pesto. Brands vary, but it is a very useful store-cupboard standby to stir into hot pasta and soups.

Pesto: fresh
Some supermarkets produce their own 'fresh' pesto, sold in tubs in the chilled cabinet. This is infinitely superior to the bottled variety, although your own freshly made pesto will be even better.

Pesto: red
A commercial sauce made from tomatoes and red peppers to stir into hot pasta or soups.

Tomato pasta sauce
Again, a good standby or base for a quick meal. Vary by adding chopped anchovies and olives, or pour over freshly cooked stuffed pasta.

Tomato purée (paste)
An essential if you are making a sauce from insipid fresh tomatoes! It will intensify any tomato-based sauce and will help thicken meat sauces. It will also make tomato pasta if added to the basic ingredients.

Tomatoes: canned plum
No store-cupboard should be without these – invaluable for making any tomato sauce or stew when good fresh tomatoes are not available.

Tomatoes: canned chopped
Usually made from Italian plum tomatoes which have a fuller flavour than most, these are the heart of a good tomato sauce if you cannot find really ripe red tasty fresh tomatoes.

Tomatoes: passata
A useful store-cupboard ingredient, this is pulped tomato that has been strained to remove the seeds. It makes a good base for a tomato sauce, though chopped canned tomatoes can also be used.

Tomatoes: sun-dried in oil
These tomatoes are drained and chopped and added to tomato-based dishes to give a deeper, almost roasted tomato flavour.

Left: *There are many ready-prepared sauces and pastes available. From top left: passata, salted anchovies, mushroom paste, olive paste, tomato purée (paste), chopped tomato, carbonara sauce, canned plum tomatoes, capers, tomato pasta sauce, red pesto, pesto, fresh pesto, sun-dried tomatoes in oil, chopped garlic.*

Eastern Pasta

Various forms of noodle or pasta exist outside Europe. They are found mainly in China and Japan, but also throughout Malaysia, Hong Kong and the rest of the Far East, including parts of India and Tibet.

This pasta, usually in noodle form and often enhanced with a sprinkling of vegetables or fish, adds variety to the sometimes monotonous staple diet of rice and beans eaten by the poorer sections of the population. Some types of pasta are used to give bulk to soups; others are eaten as a filling dish to stave off hunger during the day. They are made from the staple crops of each region – whether rice flour, soya bean flour or potato flour – and are cooked in different ways: some are soaked and then fried, some are boiled and fried and some are rolled out and stuffed like ravioli, but most are simply boiled. Some turn transparent when cooked.

Oriental egg noodles are usually made with wheat flour and can be treated in the same way as ordinary Western pasta. Buckwheat and fresh wholemeal (wholewheat) noodles are similarly cooked. Fresh white noodles do not contain egg but are cooked in the same way as egg noodles. Some dried egg noodles come in discs or blocks and are 'cooked' by immersion in boiling water in which they are then left to soak for a few minutes. As with Western pasta, oriental noodles can be flavoured with other ingredients such as prawns (shrimp), carrot and spinach. Won-ton skins, like thin squares of rolled-out pasta, are used for stuffing and making different filled shapes. Although oriental pasta is available in a variety of long noodle types, it doesn't seem to be made into the shapes we are used to seeing in Europe and America: you will often find it wound into balls and beautifully packaged.

Above: *Eastern noodles include (from top left, clockwise) Oriental rice flour noodles, rice vermicelli, rice stick noodles, hand-made amoy flour vermicelli, medium egg noodles, fresh brown mein, egg noodles, rice stick vermicelli, fresh thin egg noodles, Japanese wheat flour noodles, Ho Fan vermicelli, spinach vegetable noodles, carrot vegetable noodles, won ton skins, wheat flour noodles, fresh white mein, buckwheat noodles, shrimp egg noodles.*

Basic Sauce Ingredients

Clams
These tiny shellfish are used to make sauces and soups. Fresh cockles are a good substitute, as are canned clams in brine.

Dolcelatte
An Italian, blue-veined, creamy cheese used in sauces and fillings.

Feta
Feta is firm and crumbly with a salty taste from the brine in which it is preserved.

Gorgonzola
An Italian, blue-veined, semi-soft cheese with a piquant flavour. Used in sauces and stuffings.

Italian sausages
Meaty, highly seasoned fresh sausages used to make quick sauces and stuffings.

Mediterranean prawns (shrimp)
Raw or cooked, these large prawns have more flavour than smaller varieties.

Mussels
As with clams, mussels are best fresh, but frozen cooked ones can be substituted.

Olives
Used in sauces to add richness, black olives have more flavour than the green kind.

Onions
Spanish onions add sweetness and red or purple types add a mild flavour and attractive colour.

Pancetta
Italian streaky bacon sold smoked or unsmoked, sliced or in a piece, to add flavour to sauces.

Parmesan
A hard cheese for grating and serving with pasta, made from semi-skimmed unpasteurized cow's milk.

Peppers: red and yellow
Red and yellow peppers make a delicious addition to a sauce and are good with cold pasta salad.

Pine nuts
These small creamy-coloured nuts are essential in pesto.

Pistachios
Pale green nuts from the Middle East which are used in sweet and savoury dishes.

Ricotta
An Italian whey cheese which is soft and creamy. It is especially good in sweet or savoury fillings.

Smoked salmon
Cold smoked salmon can be thinly sliced and added to sauces and fillings.

Spinach
Spinach is an iron-rich, leafy, green vegetable mainly used to flavour and colour pasta dough.

Tomatoes
Choose only really ripe tomatoes – plum if possible. Miniature or cherry tomatoes make a good addition to sauces.

Walnuts
Walnuts are used in sweet and savoury dishes. They are also used in walnut pesto.

black olives

smoked salmon

pancetta

spinach

Italian sausages

feta

Parmesan

red and yellow (bell) peppers

Gorgonzola

Dolcelatte

onions

mussels

ricotta

pistachios

clams

pine nuts

pear tomatoes

cherry tomatoes

plum tomato

walnuts

Mediterranean
prawns (shrimp)

Equipment

To make pasta, a bare minimum of equipment is needed – practised hands would say that only a clean table top and a rolling pin were necessary. However, there are several gadgets to make pasta making easier and less hard work.

Bowls
A set of bowls is useful for mixing, whisking and so on.

Chopping board
A hygienic nylon board is recommended for cutting and chopping.

Colander
A large colander is essential for draining cooked pasta quickly.

Cook's knife
A large all-purpose cook's knife is essential for cutting pasta and for chopping.

Flour dredger
Useful for dusting pasta with small amounts of flour.

Large metal spoon
For folding in and serving sauces.

Measuring spoons
For accurately measuring quantities of ingredients.

Pasta machine or roller
Vital for kneading, rolling and cutting pasta – a real labour-saver. Attachments for other shapes are available.

Pasta or pastry wheel
For cutting pasta with a decorated edge, such as pasta bows.

Pastry brush
For removing excess flour from pasta and for brushing pasta with water, milk or beaten egg to seal.

Perforated spoon
Useful for draining small amounts of food.

Pestle and mortar
For hand-grinding pesto and crushing black peppercorns.

Ravioli cutter
For cutting or stamping out individual raviolis; can be round or square. A selection of pastry cutters will serve the same purpose.

Ravioli tray (raviolatore)
For making sheets of ravioli quickly and neatly – with practice!

Rolling pin
Pasta pins are available in specialist shops. These are long, thin and tapered at each end, but you have to be quite adept to use them. An ordinary heavy wooden rolling pin will do.

Small grater
For freshly grating nutmeg and Parmesan cheese.

Vegetable knife
For preparing vegetables and paring lemons, and for delicate work.

Vegetable peeler (parer)
For shaving Parmesan cheese and chocolate.

Whisk
Essential for beating eggs thoroughly and combining sauces smoothly.

bowls

pasta machine

cook's knife

measuring spoons

flour dredger

rolling pin

pestle and mortar

perforated spoon

large metal spoon

cutters

colander

chopping board

vegetable knife

vegetable peeler

pastry brush

metal whisk

pastry wheel

small grater

ravioli cutter

ravioli tray

To Cook Pasta

1 Throw the pasta into a large pan of boiling salted water. Stir once to prevent sticking. The addition of 15 ml/1 tbsp vegetable or olive oil will help to stop the water boiling over and prevent the pasta from sticking. *Do not cover* or the water will boil over.

2 Quickly bring the pasta back to a rolling boil and boil until *al dente* (literally 'to the tooth') – the pasta should be just firm to the bite. It should not have a hard centre or be very floppy.

3 Quickly drain the pasta well, using a large colander or sieve (strainer). Immediately rinse the pasta with boiling water to wash off any starch and to prevent the pasta from sticking together. At this stage you can toss the pasta in a little olive oil or butter if not dressing with the sauce immediately. Serve hot pasta straight away. It is up to you whether you toss the pasta with the sauce before serving or serve it with the sauce on top.

COOKING TIMES FOR FRESH AND DRIED PASTA

Calculate the cooking time from the moment the water returns to the boil after the pasta has been added.

Unfilled pasta
Fresh: 2–3 minutes, though some very thin pasta is ready as soon as the water returns to the boil.
Dried: 8–12 minutes, but keep checking as this is only a guide.

Filled pasta
Fresh: 8–10 minutes.
Dried: 15–20 minutes.

Basic Pasta Dough

Allow 200 g/7 oz/1¾ cups plain white (all-purpose) flour, pinch of salt and 15 ml/1 tbsp olive oil to 2 eggs (size 2) for 3–4 servings, depending on the required size of portion.

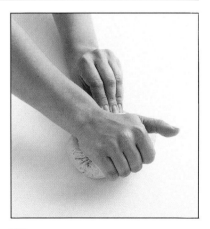

1 Sift the flour and salt on to a clean work surface and make a well in the centre with your fist.

2 Pour the beaten eggs and oil into the well. Gradually mix the eggs into the flour with the fingers of one hand.

3 Knead the pasta until smooth, wrap and allow to rest for at least 30 minutes before attempting to roll out. The pasta will be much more elastic after resting.

Using a Food Processor

1 Sift the flour into the bowl and add a pinch of salt.

2 Pour in the beaten eggs and oil and any chosen flavouring, and process until the dough begins to come together.

3 Tip out the dough and knead until smooth. Wrap and rest for 30 minutes. Use as required.

Using a Pasta Machine

1 Feed the rested dough several times through the highest setting first, then reducing the settings until the required thickness is achieved.

2 A special cutter will produce fettuccine or tagliatelle.

3 A narrower cutter will produce spaghetti or tagliarini.

COOK'S TIP

These are only guidelines: depending on the air humidity, the type of flour and so on, you may have to add more flour. The dough must not be too soft – it should be quite hard to knead. Too much extra flour will make the pasta tough and taste floury!

WATER NEEDED TO COOK PASTA

4 litres/7 pints/4½ quarts water plus 45 ml/3 tbsp salt for every 300–450 g/11 oz–1 lb/3–4 cups dried pasta or 300–450 g/11 oz–1 lb fresh pasta. This will prevent the pasta from sticking.

FLAVOURED PASTA

Tomato Pasta
Add 30 ml/2 tbsp tomato paste to the flour. Use about 1½ eggs.

Beetroot Pasta
Add 30 ml/2 tbsp grated cooked beetroot to the flour. Use about 1½ eggs.

Saffron Pasta
Soak a sachet of powdered saffron in 30 ml/2 tbsp hot water for 15 minutes. Use 1½ eggs and whisk the saffron water into them.

Herb Pasta
Add 45 ml/3 tbsp chopped fresh herbs to the flour.

Wholemeal Pasta
Use 150 g/5 oz/1¼ cups wholemeal flour sifted with 25 g/1 oz/¼ cup plain white (all-purpose) flour and 2 eggs.

Macaroni

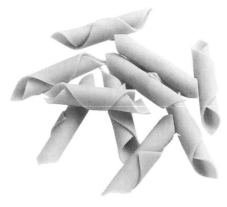

Macaroni is the generic name for any hollow pasta. This method is for making garganelle.

1 Cut squares of pasta dough using a sharp knife on a floured surface.

2 Wrap the squares around a pencil or chopstick on the diagonal to form tubes. Slip off and allow to dry slightly.

SPINACH PASTA

Use 150 g/5 oz frozen leaf spinach, cooked and squeezed of moisture, pinch of salt, 2 eggs, about 200 g/ 7 oz 1¾ cups plain white (all-purpose) flour, or a little more if the pasta is sticky. Proceed as for Basic Pasta Dough, but liquidize the spinach with the eggs to give a fine texture.

Tagliatelle

Tagliatelle can also be made with a pasta machine, but it is fairly straightforward to make it by hand.

1 Roll up the floured pasta dough like a Swiss (jelly) roll.

2 Cut the roll into thin slices with a sharp knife. Immediately unravel the slices to reveal the pasta ribbons. To make tagliarini, cut the slices 3 mm/⅛ in thick.

3 To make pappardelle, using a serrated pastry wheel, cut out wide ribbons from the rolled pasta dough.

Tortellini

Tortellini or 'little twists' can be made with meat or vegetarian fillings and served with sauce or in a soup.

1 Using a round biscuit (cookie) cutter, stamp out rounds of pasta.

2 Pipe or spoon the chosen filling into the middle of each round.

3 Brush the edges with beaten egg and fold the round into a crescent shape, excluding all the air. Bend the 2 corners round to meet each other and press well to seal. Repeat with the remaining dough. Leave to dry on a floured tea (dish) towel for 30 minutes before cooking.

SPINACH, RICOTTA AND PARMESAN FILLING FOR STUFFED PASTA
Serves 4–6

450 g/1 lb frozen spinach, thawed and squeezed dry
½ tsp freshly grated nutmeg
5 ml/1 tsp salt
freshly ground black pepper
175 g/6 oz/¾ cup fresh ricotta or curd (cottage) cheese
25 g/1 oz/¼ cup freshly grated Parmesan cheese

Place all the ingredients in a food processor and process until smooth. Use as required.

Ravioli

Although ravioli can be bought ready made, the very best is made at home. Serve with sauce or in a soup.

1 Cut the dough in half and wrap one portion in clear film (plastic wrap). Roll out the pasta thinly to a rectangle on a lightly floured surface. Cover with a clean damp tea (dish) towel and repeat with the remaining pasta. Pipe small mounds (about 5 ml/1 tsp) of filling in even rows, spacing them at 4 cm/1 ½ in intervals, across one piece of the dough. Brush the spaces between the filling with egg.

2 Using a rolling pin, lift the remaining sheet of pasta over the dough with the filling. Press down firmly between the pockets of filling, pushing out any air.

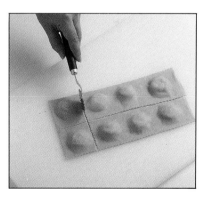

3 Cut into squares with a serrated ravioli cutter or sharp knife. Transfer to a floured tea towel and rest for 1 hour before cooking.

Minestrone

A classic substantial winter soup originally from Milan, but found in various versions around the Mediterranean coasts of Italy and France. Cut the vegetables as roughly or as small as you like. Add freshly grated Parmesan cheese just before serving.

Serves 6–8

INGREDIENTS
225 g/8 oz/2 cups dried haricot
   (navy) beans
30 ml/2 tbsp olive oil
50 g/2 oz smoked streaky bacon,
   diced
2 large onions, sliced
2 garlic cloves, crushed
2 medium carrots, diced
3 celery sticks, sliced
400 g/14 oz canned chopped
   tomatoes
2.25 litres/4 pints/10 cups beef stock
350 g/12 oz potatoes, diced
175 g/6 oz/1½ cups small pasta
   shapes (macaroni, stars, shells, etc)
225 g/8 oz green cabbage, thinly
   sliced
175 g/6 oz fine green beans, sliced
100 g/4 oz/¾ cup frozen peas
45 ml/3 tbsp chopped fresh parsley
salt and pepper
freshly grated Parmesan cheese,
   to serve

celery

cabbage

carrots

pasta shapes

onions

garlic

green beans

bacon

1 Cover the beans with cold water and leave to soak overnight.

2 Heat the oil in a large saucepan and add the bacon, onions and garlic. Cover and cook gently for 5 minutes, stirring occasionally, until soft.

3 Add the carrots and celery and cook for 2–3 minutes until softening.

4 Drain the beans and add to the pan with the tomatoes and stock. Cover and simmer for 2–2½ hours, until the beans are tender.

5 Add the potatoes 30 minutes before the soup is finished.

VARIATION

To make Soupe au Pistou from the South of France, stir in a basil, garlic and pine nut sauce (pesto or pistou) just before serving.

6 Add the pasta, cabbage, beans, peas and parsley 15 minutes before the soup is ready. Season to taste and serve with a bowl of freshly grated Parmesan cheese.

Italian Bean and Pasta Soup

A thick and hearty soup which, followed by bread and cheese, makes a substantial lunch.

Serves 6

INGREDIENTS

175 g/6 oz/1½ cups dried haricot (navy) beans, soaked overnight in cold water

1.75 litres/3 pints/7½ cups chicken stock or water

100 g/4 oz/1 cup medium pasta shells

60 ml/4 tbsp olive oil, plus extra to serve

2 garlic cloves, crushed

60 ml/4 tbsp chopped fresh parsley

salt and pepper

parsley

haricot (navy) beans

pasta shells

garlic

1 Drain the beans and place in a large saucepan with the stock or water. Simmer, half-covered, for 2–2½ hours or until tender.

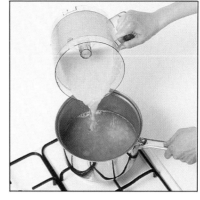

2 Liquidize half the beans and a little of their cooking liquid, then stir into the remaining beans in the pan.

3 Add the pasta and simmer gently for 15 minutes until tender. (Add extra water or stock if the soup seems too thick.)

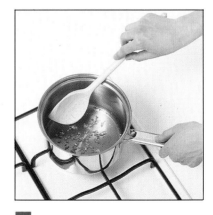

4 Heat the oil in a small pan and fry the garlic until golden. Stir into the soup with the parsley and season well with salt and pepper. Ladle into individual bowls and drizzle each with a little extra olive oil.

Courgette Soup with Small Pasta Shells

A pretty, fresh-tasting soup which could be made using cucumber instead of courgettes (zucchini).

Serves 4–6

INGREDIENTS
60 ml/4 tbsp olive or sunflower oil
2 medium onions, finely chopped
1.5 litres/2½ pints/6¼ cups chicken
   stock
900 g/2 lb courgettes (zucchini)
100 g/4 oz/1 cup small soup pasta
fresh lemon juice
salt and pepper
30 ml/2 tbsp chopped fresh chervil
soured cream, to serve

courgettes (zucchini)

onion

soup pasta

chervil

1 Heat the oil in a large saucepan and add the onions. Cover and cook gently for about 20 minutes until very soft but not coloured, stirring occasionally.

2 Add the stock and bring to the boil.

3 Meanwhile grate the courgettes and stir into the boiling stock with the pasta. Turn down the heat and simmer for 15 minutes until the pasta is tender. Season to taste with lemon juice, salt and pepper.

4 Stir in the chervil and add a swirl of soured cream before serving.

COOK'S TIP
If no fresh stock is available, instead of using a stock cube, use canned chicken or beef consommé instead.

Provençal Fish Soup with Pasta

This colourful soup has all the flavours of the Mediterranean.
Serve it as a main course for a deliciously filling lunch.

Serves 4

INGREDIENTS
30 ml/2 tbsp olive oil
1 medium onion, sliced
1 garlic clove, crushed
1 leek, sliced
225 g/8 oz canned chopped tomatoes
pinch of Mediterranean herbs
¼ tsp saffron threads (optional)
100 g/4 oz/1 cup small pasta
salt and pepper
about 8 live mussels
450 g/1 lb filleted and skinned white
    fish (cod, plaice, monkfish)

ROUILLE
2 garlic cloves, crushed
1 canned pimento, drained and
    chopped
15 ml/1 tbsp fresh white breadcrumbs
60 ml/4 tbsp mayonnaise
toasted French bread, to serve

pasta

white fish

garlic

onion

mussels

leek

1 Heat the oil in a large saucepan and add the onion, garlic and leek. Cover and cook gently for 5 minutes, stirring occasionally until soft.

2 Pour in 1 litre/1¾ pints/4½ cups water, the tomatoes, herbs, saffron and pasta. Season with salt and pepper and cook for 15–20 minutes.

3 Scrub the mussels and pull off the 'beards'. Discard any that will not close when sharply tapped: they are almost certainly dead.

4 Cut the fish into bite-sized chunks and add to the soup, placing the mussels on top. Simmer with the lid on for 5–10 minutes until the mussels open and the fish is just cooked. (If any mussels fail to open, discard them.)

5 To make the *rouille*, pound the garlic, canned pimento and breadcrumbs together in a pestle and mortar (or in a food processor). Stir in the mayonnaise and season well.

6 Spread the toasted French bread with the *rouille* and serve with the soup.

Chicken Vermicelli Soup with Egg Shreds

This soup is very quick and easy – you can add all sorts of extra ingredients to vary the taste, using up lurking left-overs such as spring onions (scallions), mushrooms, a few prawns (shrimp), chopped salami and so on.

Serves 4–6

INGREDIENTS

3 large eggs
30 ml/2 tbsp chopped fresh coriander or parsley
1.5 litres/2½ pints/6¼ cups good chicken stock or canned consommé
100 g/4 oz/1 cup dried vermicelli or angel hair pasta
100 g/4 oz cooked chicken breast, sliced
salt and pepper

vermicelli

eggs   *chicken breast*

coriander

THAI CHICKEN SOUP

To make a Thai variation, use Chinese rice noodles instead of pasta. Stir ½ tsp dried lemon grass, 2 small whole fresh chillies and 60 ml/4 tbsp coconut milk into the stock. Add 4 sliced spring onions (scallions) and plenty of chopped fresh coriander.

1 First make the egg shreds. Whisk the eggs together in a small bowl and stir in the coriander or parsley.

2 Heat a small non-stick frying pan (skillet) and pour in 2–3 tbsp egg, swirling to cover the base evenly. Cook until set. Repeat until all the mixture is used up.

3 Roll each pancake up and slice thinly into shreds. Set aside.

4 Bring the stock to the boil and add the pasta, breaking it up into short lengths. Cook for 3–5 minutes until the pasta is almost tender, then add the chicken, salt and pepper. Heat through for 2–3 minutes, then stir in the egg shreds. Serve immediately.

Creamy Parmesan and Cauliflower Soup with Pasta Bows

A silky smooth, mildly cheesy soup which isn't overpowered by the cauliflower. It is an elegant dinner party soup served with the crisp melba toast.

Serves 6

INGREDIENTS
1 large cauliflower
1.1 litres/2 pints/5 cups chicken or
    vegetable stock
175 g/6 oz/1½ cups pasta bows
    (farfalle)
150 ml/5 fl oz/⅔ cup single (light)
    cream or milk
freshly grated nutmeg
pinch of cayenne pepper
60 ml/4 tbsp freshly grated Parmesan
    cheese
salt and pepper

MELBA TOAST
3–4 slices day-old white bread
freshly grated Parmesan cheese, for
    sprinkling
¼ tsp paprika

cauliflower

pasta bows

Parmesan cheese

nutmeg

1 Cut the leaves and central stalk away from the cauliflower and discard. Divide the cauliflower into florets (flowerets).

2 Bring the stock to the boil and add the cauliflower. Simmer for about 10 minutes or until very soft. Remove the cauliflower with a perforated spoon and place in a food processor.

3 Add the pasta to the stock and simmer for 10 minutes until tender. Drain, reserve the pasta, and pour the liquid over the cauliflower in the food processor. Add the cream or milk, nutmeg and cayenne to the cauliflower. Blend until smooth, then press through a sieve (strainer). Stir in the cooked pasta. Reheat the soup and stir in the Parmesan. Taste and adjust the seasoning.

4 Meanwhile make the melba toast. Pre-heat the oven to 180°C/350°F/gas mark 4. Toast the bread lightly on both sides. Quickly cut off the crusts and split each slice in half horizontally. Scrape off any doughy bits and sprinkle with Parmesan and paprika. Place on a baking sheet and bake in the oven for 10–15 minutes or until uniformly golden. Serve with the soup.

Pasta with Roasted Pepper and Tomato Sauce

Add other vegetables such as French beans or courgettes (zucchini) or even chick peas (garbanzos) to make this sauce more substantial.

Serves 4

INGREDIENTS
2 medium red (bell) peppers
2 medium yellow (bell) peppers
45 ml/3 tbsp olive oil
1 medium onion, sliced
2 garlic cloves, crushed
½ tsp mild chilli powder
400 g/14 oz canned chopped plum
    tomatoes
salt and pepper
450 g/1 lb/4 cups dried pasta shells or
    spirals
freshly grated Parmesan cheese, to
    serve

peppers

pasta shells

onion

garlic

1 Pre-heat the oven to 200°C/400°F/gas mark 6. Place the peppers on a baking sheet or in a roasting tin (roasting pan) and bake for about 20 minutes or until beginning to char. Alternatively grill (broil) the peppers, turning frequently.

2 Rub the skins off the peppers under cold water. Halve, remove the seeds and roughly chop the flesh.

3 Heat the oil in a medium saucepan and add the onion and garlic. Cook gently for 5 minutes until soft and golden.

4 Stir in the chilli powder, cook for 2 minutes, then add the tomatoes and peppers. Bring to the boil and simmer for 10–15 minutes until slightly thickened and reduced. Season to taste.

5 Cook the pasta in plenty of boiling salted water according to the manufacturer's instructions. Drain well and toss with the sauce. Serve piping hot with lots of Parmesan cheese.

Tagliatelle with Walnut Sauce

An unusual sauce which would make this a spectacular dinner party starter.

Serves 4–6

INGREDIENTS

2 thick slices wholemeal (whole-wheat) bread
300 ml/10 fl oz/1¼ cups milk
275 g/10 oz/2½ cups walnut pieces
1 garlic clove, crushed
50 g/2 oz/½ cup freshly grated Parmesan cheese
90 ml/6 tbsp olive oil, plus extra for tossing the pasta
salt and pepper
150 ml/5 fl oz/⅓ cup double (heavy) cream (optional)
450 g/1 lb tagliatelle
30 ml/2 tbsp chopped fresh parsley

tagliatelle

parsley

garlic

walnut pieces

VARIATION

Add 100 g/4 oz/¾ cup stoned (pitted) black olives to the food processor with the other ingredients for a richer, more piquant sauce. The Greek-style olives have the most flavour.

1 Cut the crusts off the bread and soak in the milk until the milk is all absorbed.

2 Pre-heat the oven to 190°C/375°F/gas mark 5. Spread the walnuts on a baking sheet and toast in the oven for 5 minutes. Leave to cool.

3 Place the bread, walnuts, garlic, Parmesan cheese and olive oil in a food processor and blend until smooth. Season to taste with salt and pepper. Stir in the cream, if using.

4 Cook the pasta in plenty of boiling salted water, drain and toss with a little olive oil. Divide the pasta equally between 4 bowls and place a dollop of sauce on each portion. Sprinkle with parsley.

Stir-fried Vegetables with Pasta

This is a colourful Chinese-style dish, easily prepared using pasta instead of Chinese noodles.

Serves 4

INGREDIENTS
1 medium carrot
175 g/6 oz small courgettes (zucchini)
175 g/6 oz runner or other green beans
175 g/6 oz baby sweetcorn
450 g/1 lb ribbon pasta such as tagliatelle
salt
30 ml/2 tbsp corn oil, plus extra for tossing the pasta
1 cm/½ in piece fresh root ginger, peeled and finely chopped
2 garlic cloves, finely chopped
90 ml/6 tbsp yellow bean sauce
6 spring onions (scallions), sliced into 2.5 cm/1 in lengths
30 ml/2 tbsp dry sherry
5 ml/1 tsp sesame seeds

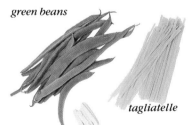

green beans

tagliatelle

baby sweetcorn

root ginger

spring onions (scallions)

courgettes (zucchini)

garlic

1 Slice the carrot and courgettes (zucchini) diagonally into chunks. Slice the beans diagonally. Cut the baby corn diagonally in half.

2 Cook the pasta in plenty of boiling salted water according to the manufacturer's instructions, drain, then rinse under hot water. Toss in a little oil.

3 Heat 30 ml/2 tbsp oil until smoking in a wok or frying pan (skillet) and add the ginger and garlic. Stir-fry for 30 seconds, then add the carrots, beans and courgettes.

4 Stir-fry for 3–4 minutes, then stir in the yellow bean sauce. Stir-fry for 2 minutes, add the spring onions (scallions), sherry and pasta and stir-fry for a further 1 minute until piping hot. Sprinkle with sesame seeds and serve immediately.

Spaghetti with Fresh Tomato Sauce

The heat from the pasta will release the delicious flavours of this sauce. Only use the really red and soft tomatoes – large ripe beefsteak or Marmande tomatoes are ideal. Don't be tempted to use small hard tomatoes: they have very little flavour.

Serves 4

INGREDIENTS
4 large ripe tomatoes
2 garlic cloves, finely chopped
60 ml/4 tbsp chopped fresh herbs
    such as basil, marjoram, oregano or
    parsley
150 ml/5 fl oz/⅔ cup olive oil
salt and pepper
450 g/1 lb spaghetti

olive oil

garlic

spaghetti

tomato

2 Lift out with a perforated spoon and plunge into a bowl of cold water. Peel off the skins, then dry the tomatoes on kitchen paper.

3 Halve the tomatoes and squeeze out the seeds. Chop into 6 mm/¼ in cubes and mix with the garlic, herbs, olive oil and seasoning in a non-metallic bowl. Cover and allow the flavours to mellow for at least 30 minutes.

1 Skin the tomatoes by placing in boiling water for 1 minute – no longer or they will become mushy.

4 Cook the pasta in plenty of boiling salted water.

5 Drain the pasta and mix with the sauce. Cover with a lid and leave for 2–3 minutes, toss again and serve immediately.

VARIATION

Mix 100 g/4 oz/¾ cup stoned (pitted) and chopped black Greek-style olives into the sauce just before serving.

Tagliatelle with Gorgonzola Sauce

Gorgonzola is a creamy Italian blue cheese. As an alternative you could use Danish Blue or Pipo Creme.

Serves 4

INGREDIENTS

25 g/1 oz/2 tbsp butter, plus extra for
  tossing the pasta
225 g/8 oz Gorgonzola cheese
150 ml/5 fl oz/⅔ cup double (heavy)
  or whipping cream
30 ml/2 tbsp dry vermouth
5 ml/1 tsp cornflour (cornstarch)
15 ml/1 tbsp chopped fresh sage
salt and pepper
450 g/1 lb tagliatelle

tagliatelle

Gorgonzola

sage

1 Melt 25 g/1 oz/2 tbsp butter in a heavy saucepan (it needs to be thick-based to prevent the cheese from burning). Stir in 175 g/6 oz crumbled Gorgonzola cheese and stir over a very gentle heat for 2–3 minutes until the cheese is melted.

2 Pour in the cream, vermouth and cornflour, whisking well to amalgamate. Stir in the chopped sage, then taste and season. Cook, whisking all the time, until the sauce boils and thickens. Set aside.

3 Boil the pasta in plenty of salted water according to the manufacturer's instructions. Drain well and toss with a little butter.

4 Reheat the sauce gently, whisking well. Divide the pasta between 4 serving bowls, top with the sauce and sprinkle over the remaining cheese. Serve immediately.

Pasta with Tomato and Cream Sauce

Here pasta is served with a deliciously rich version of ordinary tomato sauce.

Serves 4–6

INGREDIENTS
30 ml/2 tbsp olive oil
2 garlic cloves, crushed
400 g/14 oz canned chopped
    tomatoes
150 ml/5 fl oz/⅔ cup double (heavy)
    or whipping cream
30 ml/2 tbsp chopped fresh herbs
    such as basil, oregano or parsley
salt and pepper
450 g/1 lb/4 cups pasta, any variety

chopped tomatoes

olive oil

pasta

parsley

garlic

1 Heat the oil in a medium saucepan, add the garlic and cook for 2 minutes until golden.

2 Stir in the tomatoes, bring to the boil and simmer uncovered for 20 minutes, stirring occasionally to prevent sticking. The sauce is ready when you can see the oil separating on top.

3 Add the cream, bring slowly to the boil again and simmer until slightly thickened. Stir in the herbs, taste and season well.

4 Cook the pasta in plenty of boiling salted water according to the manufacturer's instructions. Drain well and toss with the sauce. Serve piping hot, sprinkled with extra herbs if liked.

COOK'S TIP

If you are really in a hurry, buy a good ready-made tomato sauce and simply stir in the cream and simmer until thickened.

Rigatoni with Garlic Crumbs

A hot and spicy dish – halve the quantity of chilli if you like a milder flavour. The bacon is an addition for meat-eaters; leave it out or replace it with sliced mushrooms, if you prefer.

Serves 4–6

INGREDIENTS
45 ml/3 tbsp olive oil
2 shallots, chopped
8 rashers (slices) streaky bacon,
   chopped (optional)
10 ml/2 tsp crushed dried chillies
400 g/14 oz canned chopped
   tomatoes with garlic and herbs
6 slices white bread
100 g/4 oz/½ cup butter
2 garlic cloves, chopped
450 g/1 lb/4 cups rigatoni
salt and pepper

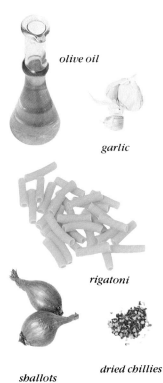

olive oil

garlic

rigatoni

shallots　　*dried chillies*

1 Heat the oil in a medium saucepan and fry the shallots and bacon gently for 6–8 minutes until golden. Add the dried chillies and chopped tomatoes, half-cover and simmer for 20 minutes.

2 Meanwhile cut the crusts off the bread and discard them. Reduce the bread to crumbs in a food processor.

3 Heat the butter in a frying pan (skillet), add the garlic and breadcrumbs and stir-fry until golden and crisp. (Don't let the crumbs catch and burn or the dish will be ruined!)

4 Cook the pasta in boiling salted water according to the manufacturer's instructions. Drain well.

5 Toss the pasta with the tomato sauce and divide between 4 serving bowls.

6 Sprinkle with the crumbs and serve immediately.

Tortellini with Cream, Butter and Cheese

This is an indulgent but quick alternative to macaroni cheese. Meat-eaters could stir in some ham or pepperoni, though it's quite delicious as it is!

Serves 4–6

INGREDIENTS
450 g/1 lb/4 cups fresh tortellini
salt and pepper
50 g/2 oz/4 tbsp butter
300 ml/10 fl oz/1¼ cups double
  (heavy) cream
100 g/4 oz piece fresh Parmesan
  cheese
freshly grated nutmeg

tortellini

Parmesan cheese

nutmeg

COOK'S TIP

Ring the changes with different cheeses, but don't try to use single (light) cream or it will curdle.

1 Cook the pasta in plenty of boiling salted water according to the manufacturer's instructions.

2 Meanwhile melt the butter in a medium saucepan and stir in the cream. Bring to the boil and cook for 2–3 minutes until slightly thickened.

3 Grate the Parmesan cheese and stir 75 g/3 oz/¾ cup into the sauce until melted. Season to taste with salt, pepper and nutmeg. Pre-heat the grill (broiler).

4 Drain the pasta well and spoon into a buttered heatproof serving dish. Pour over the sauce, sprinkle over the remaining cheese and place under the grill until brown and bubbling. Serve immediately.

Baked Tortellini with Three Cheeses

Serve this straight out of the oven while the cheese is still runny. If smoked mozzarella cheese is not available, try using a smoked German cheese or even grated smoked Cheddar.

Serves 4–6

INGREDIENTS
450 g/1 lb/4 cups fresh tortellini
salt and pepper
2 eggs
350 g/12 oz/1½ cups ricotta or curd
  (cottage) cheese
25 g/1 oz/2 tbsp butter
25 g/1 oz fresh basil leaves
100 g/4 oz smoked cheese, such as
  mozzarella or Cheddar, grated
60 ml/4 tbsp freshly grated Parmesan
  cheese

tortellini

smoked cheese

basil

eggs

1 Pre-heat the oven to 190°C/375°F/ gas mark 5. Cook the tortellini in plenty of boiling salted water according to the manufacturer's instructions. Drain well.

2 Beat the eggs with the ricotta cheese and season well with salt and pepper. Use the butter to grease an ovenproof dish. Spoon in half the tortellini, pour over half the ricotta mixture and cover with half the basil leaves.

3 Cover with the smoked cheese and remaining basil. Top with the rest of the tortellini and spread over the remaining ricotta.

4 Sprinkle evenly with the Parmesan cheese. Bake in the oven for 35–45 minutes or until golden-brown and bubbling.

Pasta Shells with Tomatoes and Rocket

This pretty-coloured pasta dish relies for its success on a salad green called rocket (arugula). Available in large supermarkets, it is a leaf easily grown in the garden or a window box and tastes slightly peppery.

Serves 4

INGREDIENTS
450 g/1 lb/4 cups pasta shells
salt and pepper
450 g/1 lb ripe cherry tomatoes
45 ml/3 tbsp olive oil
Parmesan cheese, to serve
75 g/3 oz fresh rocket

olive oil

pasta shells

cherry tomatoes

Parmesan cheese

rocket (arugula)

1 Cook the pasta in plenty of boiling salted water according to the manufacturer's instructions. Drain well.

2 Halve the tomatoes. Trim, wash and dry the rocket (arugula).

3 Heat the oil in a large saucepan, add the tomatoes and cook for barely 1 minute. The tomatoes should only just heat through and not disintegrate.

4 Shave the Parmesan cheese using a rotary vegetable peeler.

5 Add the pasta, then the rocket. Carefully stir to mix and heat through. Season well with salt and freshly ground black pepper. Serve immediately with plenty of shaved Parmesan cheese.

Pasta Tossed with Grilled Vegetables

A hearty dish to be eaten with crusty bread and washed down with a robust red wine. Try barbecuing the vegetables for a really smoky flavour.

Serves 4

INGREDIENTS
1 medium aubergine (eggplant)
2 medium courgettes (zucchini)
1 medium red (bell) pepper
8 garlic cloves, unpeeled
about 150 ml/5 fl oz/⅔ cup good olive
  oil
salt and pepper
450 g/1 lb ribbon pasta (pappardelle)
few sprigs fresh thyme, to garnish

olive oil

courgettes (zucchini)

aubergine (eggplant)

ribbon pasta

thyme

garlic

pepper

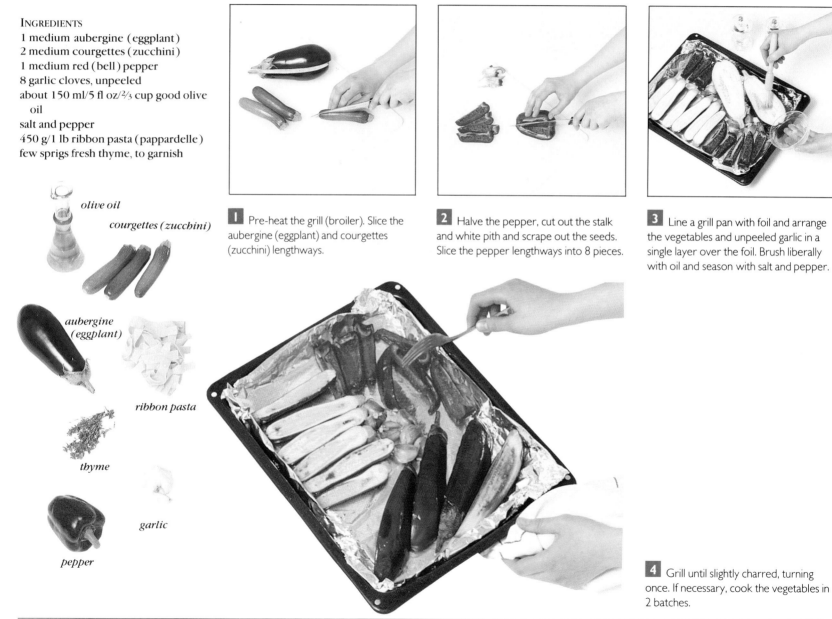

1 Pre-heat the grill (broiler). Slice the aubergine (eggplant) and courgettes (zucchini) lengthways.

2 Halve the pepper, cut out the stalk and white pith and scrape out the seeds. Slice the pepper lengthways into 8 pieces.

3 Line a grill pan with foil and arrange the vegetables and unpeeled garlic in a single layer over the foil. Brush liberally with oil and season with salt and pepper.

4 Grill until slightly charred, turning once. If necessary, cook the vegetables in 2 batches.

5 Cool the garlic, remove the charred skins and halve. Toss the vegetables with olive oil and keep warm.

6 Meanwhile cook the pasta in plenty of boiling salted water according to the manufacturer's instructions. Drain well and toss with the grilled vegetables. Serve immediately garnished with sprigs of thyme and accompanied by plenty of country bread.

Green Pasta with Avocado Sauce

This is an unusual sauce with a pale green colour, studded with red tomato. It has a luxurious velvety texture. The sauce is rather rich, so you don't need too much of it.

Serves 6

INGREDIENTS
3 ripe tomatoes
2 large ripe avocados
25 g/1 oz/2 tbsp butter, plus extra for
   tossing the pasta
1 garlic clove, crushed
450 ml/12 fl oz/1½ cups double
   (heavy) cream
salt and pepper
dash of Tabasco sauce
450 g/1 lb green tagliatelle
freshly grated Parmesan cheese
60 ml/4 tbsp soured cream

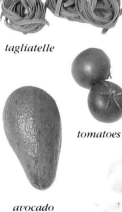

tagliatelle

tomatoes

avocado

garlic

1 Halve the tomatoes and remove the cores. Squeeze out the seeds and cut the tomatoes into dice. Set aside.

2 Halve the avocados, take out the stones (pits) and peel. Roughly chop up the flesh.

3 Melt the butter in a saucepan and add the garlic. Cook for 1 minute, then add the cream and chopped avocados. Raise the heat, stirring constantly to break up the avocados.

4 Add the diced tomatoes and season to taste with salt, pepper and a little Tabasco sauce. Keep warm.

5 Cook the pasta in plenty of boiling salted water according to the manufacturer's instructions. Drain well and toss with a knob of butter.

6 Divide the pasta between 4 warmed bowls and spoon over the sauce. Sprinkle with grated Parmesan and top with a spoonful of soured cream.

Spaghetti with Creamy Mussel and Saffron Sauce

In this recipe the pasta is tossed with a delicious pale yellow mussel sauce, streaked with yellow threads of saffron. Powdered saffron will do just as well, but don't use turmeric – the flavour will be too strong.

Serves 4

INGREDIENTS
900 g/2 lb live mussels
150 ml/5 fl oz/⅔ cup dry white wine
2 shallots, finely chopped
25 g/1 oz/2 tbsp butter
2 garlic cloves, crushed
10 ml/2 tsp cornflour (cornstarch)
300 ml/10 fl oz/1¼ cups double (heavy) cream
pinch of saffron threads
salt and pepper
juice of ½ lemon
1 egg yolk
450 g/1 lb spaghetti
chopped fresh parsley, to garnish

spaghetti   *parsley*

mussels

garlic

shallots

1 Scrub the mussels and rinse well. Pull off any 'beards' and leave the shellfish to soak in cold water for 30 minutes. Tap each mussel sharply after this time. Any that do not close straight away are dead and should be thrown away.

2 Drain the mussels and place in a large saucepan. Add the wine and shallots, cover and cook (shaking frequently) over a high heat for 5–10 minutes until the mussels are open. If some do not open at this stage, throw them out.

3 Pass through a sieve (strainer), reserving the liquid. Remove most of the mussels from their shells. Reserve some in the shell to use as a garnish. Boil the reserved liquid rapidly in a medium saucepan until reduced by half.

4 Melt the butter in another saucepan, add the garlic and cook until golden. Stir in the cornflour (cornstarch) and gradually stir in the cooking liquid and the cream. Add the saffron and seasoning and simmer until slightly thickened.

5 Stir in lemon juice to taste, then the egg yolk and mussels. Keep warm, but do not boil.

6 Cook the pasta in plenty of boiling salted water according to the manufacturer's instructions. Drain well. Toss the mussels with the spaghetti, garnish with the reserved mussels in their shells and sprinkle with the chopped parsley. Serve immediately with lots of crusty bread.

Pasta Spirals with Pepperoni and Tomato Sauce

A warming supper dish, perfect for cold winter nights. All types of sausage are suitable, but if using raw sausages, make sure that they go in with the onion to cook thoroughly.

Serves 4

INGREDIENTS
1 medium onion
1 red (bell) pepper
1 green (bell) pepper
30 ml/2 tbsp olive oil, plus extra for
   tossing the pasta
800 g/1¾ lb canned chopped
   tomatoes
30 ml/2 tbsp tomato purée (paste)
10 ml/2 tsp paprika
175 g/6 oz pepperoni or chorizo
   (spicy sausage)
45 ml/3 tbsp chopped fresh parsley
salt and pepper
450 g/1 lb/4 cups pasta spirals
   (fusilli)

pasta spirals

pepperoni

peppers

onion

parsley

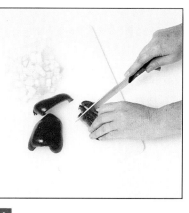

1 Chop the onion. Halve and seed the peppers, removing the cores, then cut the flesh into dice.

2 Heat the oil in a medium saucepan, add the onion and cook for 2–3 minutes until beginning to colour. Stir in the peppers, tomatoes, tomato purée (paste) and paprika, bring to the boil and simmer uncovered for 15–20 minutes until reduced and thickened.

3 Slice the pepperoni and stir into the sauce with 30 ml/2 tbsp chopped parsley. Season to taste.

4 While the sauce is simmering, cook the pasta in plenty of boiling salted water according to the manufacturer's instructions. Drain well. Toss the pasta with the remaining parsley in a little extra olive oil. Divide between warmed bowls and top with the sauce.

Spaghetti with Tomato and Clam Sauce

Small sweet clams make this a delicately succulent sauce. Cockles would make a good substitute, or even mussels. Don't be tempted to use seafood pickled in vinegar – the result will be inedible!

Serves 4

INGREDIENTS
900 g/2 lb live small clams, or 2 ×
    400 g/14 oz cans clams in brine,
    drained
90 ml/6 tbsp olive oil
2 garlic cloves, crushed
600 g/1 lb 5 oz canned chopped
    tomatoes
45 ml/3 tbsp chopped fresh parsley
salt and pepper
450 g/1 lb spaghetti

olive oil   *spaghetti*

parsley

garlic

clams

1 If using live clams, place them in a bowl of cold water and rinse several times to remove any grit or sand. Drain.

2 Heat the oil in a saucepan and add the clams. Stir over a high heat until the clams open. Throw away any that do not open. Transfer the clams to a bowl with a perforated spoon.

3 Reduce the clam juice left in the pan to almost nothing by boiling fast; this will also concentrate the flavour. Add the garlic and fry until golden. Pour in the tomatoes, bring to the boil and cook for 3–4 minutes until reduced. Stir in the clam mixture or canned clams and half the parsley and heat through. Season.

4 Cook the pasta in plenty of boiling salted water according to the manufacturer's instructions. Drain well and turn into a warm serving dish. Pour over the sauce and sprinkle with the remaining parsley.

Pasta with Tuna, Capers and Anchovies

This piquant sauce could be made without the addition of tomatoes – just heat the oil, add the other ingredients and heat through gently before tossing with the pasta.

Serves 4

INGREDIENTS

400 g/14 oz canned tuna fish in oil
30 ml/2 tbsp olive oil
2 garlic cloves, crushed
800 g/1¾ lb canned chopped
   tomatoes
6 canned anchovy fillets, drained
30 ml/2 tbsp capers in vinegar,
   drained
30 ml/2 tbsp chopped fresh basil
salt and pepper
450 g/1 lb/4 cups rigatoni, penne or
   garganelle
sprigs fresh basil, to garnish

olive oil

rigatoni

tuna fish

anchovy fillets

basil

capers

garlic

1 Drain the oil from the tuna into a saucepan, add the olive oil and heat gently until it stops 'spitting'.

2 Add the garlic and fry until golden. Stir in the tomatoes and simmer for 25 minutes until thickened.

3 Flake the tuna and cut the anchovies in half. Stir into the sauce with the capers and chopped basil. Season well.

4 Cook the pasta in plenty of boiling salted water according to the manufacturer's instructions. Drain well and toss with the sauce. Garnish with fresh basil sprigs.

Pasta Bows with Smoked Salmon and Dill

In Italy, pasta cooked with smoked salmon is becoming very fashionable. This is a quick and luxurious sauce.

Serves 4

INGREDIENTS
6 spring onions (scallions), sliced
50 g/2 oz/4 tbsp butter
90 ml/6 tbsp dry white wine or
    vermouth
450 ml/15 fl oz/2 cups double (heavy)
    cream
salt and pepper
freshly grated nutmeg
225 g/8 oz smoked salmon
30 ml/2 tbsp chopped fresh dill or
    15 ml/1 tbsp dried dillweed
freshly squeezed lemon juice
450 g/1 lb/4 cups pasta bows (farfalle)

pasta bows

lemon

spring onions (scallions)

smoked salmon

nutmeg

dill

1 Slice the spring onions (scallions) finely. Melt the butter in a saucepan and fry the spring onions for 1 minute until softened.

2 Add the wine and boil hard to reduce to about 30 ml/2 tbsp. Stir in the cream and add salt, pepper and nutmeg to taste. Bring to the boil and simmer for 2–3 minutes until slightly thickened.

3 Cut the smoked salmon into 2.5 cm/ 1 in squares and stir into the sauce with the dill. Taste and add a little lemon juice. Keep warm.

4 Cook the pasta in plenty of boiling salted water according to the manufacturer's instructions. Drain well. Toss the pasta with the sauce and serve immediately.

Prawns with Tagliatelle and Pesto in Packets

A quick and impressive dish, easy to prepare in advance and cook at the last minute. When the packets are opened, the filling smells wonderful.

Serves 4

INGREDIENTS

750 g/1½ lb medium raw prawns (shrimp), shells on
450 g/1 lb tagliatelle or similar pasta
salt and pepper
150 ml/5 fl oz/⅔ cup fresh pesto sauce or ready-made equivalent
20 ml/4 tsp olive oil
1 garlic clove, crushed
100 ml/4 fl oz/½ cup dry white wine

olive oil

tagliatelle

prawns (shrimp)

pesto sauce

garlic

1 Pre-heat the oven to 200°C/400°F/gas mark 6. Twist the heads off the prawns (shrimp) and discard.

2 Cook the tagliatelle in plenty of boiling salted water for 2 minutes only, then drain. Mix with half the pesto.

3 Cut 4 × 30 cm/12 in squares of greaseproof (baking) paper and place 5 ml/1 tsp olive oil in the centre of each. Pile equal amounts of pasta in the middle of each square.

4 Top with equal amounts of prawns and spoon the remaining pesto mixed with the crushed garlic over the prawns. Season with black pepper and sprinkle each serving with 30 ml/2 tbsp wine.

5 Brush the edges of the paper lightly with water and bring them loosely up around the filling, twisting tightly to enclose. (The parcels should look like money bags.)

6 Place the parcels on a baking sheet. Bake in the oven for 10–15 minutes. Serve immediately, allowing each person to open his/her own packet.

Rigatoni with Spicy Sausage and Tomato Sauce

This is really a cheat's Bolognese sauce using the wonderful fresh spicy sausages sold in every Italian delicatessen.

Serves 4

INGREDIENTS
450 g/1 lb fresh spicy Italian sausage
30 ml/2 tbsp olive oil
1 medium onion, chopped
450 ml/15 fl oz/2 cups passata
  (strained crushed tomatoes)
150 ml/5 fl oz/⅔ cup dry red wine
6 sun-dried tomatoes in oil, drained
salt and pepper
450 g/1 lb/4 cups rigatoni or similar
  pasta
freshly grated Parmesan cheese, to
  serve

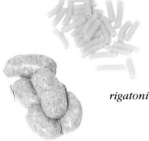

rigatoni

Italian sausage

Parmesan cheese

onion

sun-dried tomatoes

1 Squeeze the sausages out of their skins into a bowl and break up the meat.

2 Heat the oil in a medium saucepan and add the onion. Cook for 5 minutes until soft and golden. Stir in the sausagemeat, browning it all over and breaking up the lumps with a wooden spoon. Pour in the passata and the wine. Bring to the boil.

3 Slice the sun-dried tomatoes and add to the sauce. Simmer for 3 minutes until reduced, stirring occasionally. Season.

4 Cook the pasta in plenty of boiling salted water according to the manufacturer's instructions. Drain well and top with the sauce. Serve with grated Parmesan cheese.

Pasta with Fresh Tomato and Smoky Bacon Sauce

A wonderful sauce to prepare in mid-summer when the tomatoes are ripe and sweet.

Serves 4

INGREDIENTS
900 g/2 lb ripe tomatoes
6 rashers (slices) smoked streaky
   bacon
50 g/2 oz/4 tbsp butter
1 medium onion, chopped
salt and pepper
15 ml/1 tbsp chopped fresh oregano
   or 5 ml/1 tsp dried oregano
450 g/1 lb/4 cups pasta, any variety
freshly grated Parmesan cheese, to
   serve

pasta

oregano

tomatoes

onion

bacon

Parmesan cheese

1 Plunge the tomatoes into boiling water for 1 minute, then into cold water to stop them from becoming mushy. Slip off the skins. Halve the tomatoes, remove the seeds and cores and roughly chop the flesh.

2 Remove the rind from the bacon and roughly chop.

3 Melt the butter in a saucepan and add the bacon. Fry until lightly brown, then add the onion and cook gently for 5 minutes until softened. Add the tomatoes, salt, pepper and oregano. Simmer gently for 10 minutes.

4 Cook the pasta in plenty of boiling salted water according to the manufacturer's instructions. Drain well and toss with the sauce. Serve with grated Parmesan cheese.

Pasta with Prawns and Feta Cheese

This dish combines the richness of fresh prawns (shrimp) with the tartness of feta cheese. Goat's cheese could also be used.

Serves 4

INGREDIENTS
450 g/1 lb medium raw prawns
  (shrimp)
6 spring onions (scallions)
50 g/2 oz/4 tbsp butter
225 g/8 oz feta cheese
small bunch fresh chives
450 g/1 lb/4 cups penne, garganelle or
  rigatoni
salt and pepper

penne

spring onions (scallions)

feta

chives

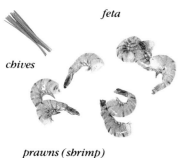

prawns (shrimp)

1 Remove the heads from the prawns (shrimp) by twisting and pulling off. Peel the prawns and discard the shells. Chop the spring onions (scallions).

2 Melt the butter in a frying pan (skillet) and stir in the prawns. When they turn pink, add the spring onions and cook gently for 1 minute.

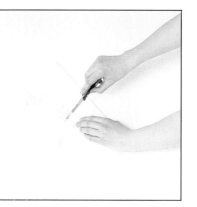

3 Cut the feta into 1 cm/½ in cubes.

4 Stir the feta cheese into the prawn mixture and season with black pepper.

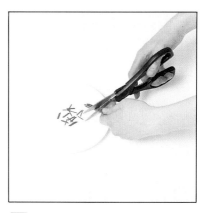

5 Cut the chives into 2.5 cm/1 in lengths and stir half into the prawns.

6 Cook the pasta in plenty of boiling salted water according to the manufacturer's instructions. Drain well, pile into a warmed serving dish and top with the sauce. Scatter with the remaining chives and serve.

Tagliatelle with Prosciutto and Parmesan

A really simple dish, prepared in minutes from the best ingredients.

Serves 4

INGREDIENTS
100 g/4 oz prosciutto
450 g/1 lb tagliatelle
salt and pepper
75 g/3 oz/6 tbsp butter
50 g/2 oz/½ cup freshly grated
    Parmesan cheese
few fresh sage leaves, to garnish

tagliatelle

sage

prosciutto

Parmesan cheese

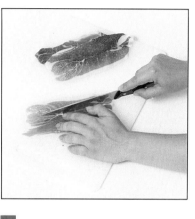

1 Cut the prosciutto into strips of the same width as the tagliatelle. Cook the pasta in plenty of boiling salted water according to manufacturer's instructions.

2 Meanwhile melt the butter gently in a saucepan, stir in the prosciutto strips and heat through, but do not fry.

3 Drain the tagliatelle well and pile into a warm serving dish.

4 Sprinkle over all the Parmesan cheese and pour over the buttery prosciutto. Season well with black pepper and garnish with the sage leaves.

Pasta with Spinach and Anchovy Sauce

Deliciously earthy, this would make a good starter or light supper dish. Add some sultanas (golden raisins) to ring the changes!

Serves 4

INGREDIENTS
900 g/2 lb fresh spinach or 550 g/
 1¼ lb frozen leaf spinach, thawed
450 g/1 lb/4 cups angel hair pasta
salt
60 ml/4 tbsp olive oil
45 ml/3 tbsp pine nuts
2 garlic cloves, crushed
6 canned anchovy fillets or whole
 salted anchovies, drained and
 chopped
butter, for tossing the pasta

olive oil

pine nuts

spinach

anchovy fillets

garlic　　*angel hair pasta*

1 Wash the spinach well and remove the tough stalks. Drain thoroughly. Place in a large saucepan with only the water that still clings to the leaves. Cover with a lid and cook over a high heat, shaking the pan occasionally, until the spinach is just wilted and still bright green. Drain.

2 Cook the pasta in plenty of boiling salted water according to the manufacturer's instructions.

3 Heat the oil in a saucepan and fry the pine nuts until golden. Remove with a perforated spoon. Add the garlic to the oil in the pan and fry until golden. Add the anchovies.

4 Stir in the spinach and cook for 2–3 minutes or until heated through. Stir in the pine nuts. Drain the pasta, toss in a little butter and turn into a warmed serving bowl. Top with the sauce and fork through roughly.

Lasagne al Forno

The classic version of this dish is pasta layered with meat sauce and creamy béchamel sauce. You could vary it by using mozzarella cheese instead of the béchamel sauce, or by mixing ricotta cheese, Parmesan and herbs together instead of the traditional meat sauce.

Serves 4–6

INGREDIENTS
about 12 sheets dried lasagne
1 recipe Bolognese Sauce
about 50 g/2 oz/½ cup freshly grated
    Parmesan cheese
tomato slices and parsley sprig, to
    garnish

BÉCHAMEL SAUCE
850 ml/1½ pints/3¾ cups milk
sliced onion, carrot, celery
few whole peppercorns
50 g/2 oz/½ cup butter
75 g/3 oz/⅔ cup plain (all-purpose)
    flour
salt and pepper
freshly grated nutmeg

1 First make the béchamel sauce. Pour the milk into a saucepan and add the vegetables and peppercorns. Bring to boiling point, remove from the heat and leave to infuse for at least 30 minutes.

2 Strain the milk into a jug. Melt the butter in the same saucepan and stir in the flour. Cook, stirring, for 2 minutes.

3 Remove from the heat and add the milk all in one go, whisk well and return to the heat. Bring to the boil, whisking all the time, then simmer for 2–3 minutes, stirring constantly until thickened. Season to taste with salt, pepper and nutmeg.

lasagne

carrot

onion

celery

Parmesan cheese

Bolognese Sauce

4 Pre-heat the oven to 180°C/350°F/ gas mark 4. If necessary, cook the sheets of lasagne in plenty of boiling salted water according to the instructions. Lift out with a perforated spoon and drain on a clean tea (dish) towel. Spoon one-third of the meat sauce into a buttered baking-dish.

5 Cover the meat sauce with 4 sheets of lasagne and spread with one-third of the béchamel sauce. Repeat twice more, finishing with a layer of béchamel sauce covering the whole top.

6 Sprinkle with Parmesan cheese and bake in the oven for about 45 minutes until brown. Serve garnished with tomato slices and a sprig of parsley.

Cannelloni al Forno

A lighter alternative to the usual beef-filled, béchamel-coated version. Fill with ricotta, onion and mushroom for a vegetarian recipe.

Serves 4–6

INGREDIENTS
450 g/1 lb/4 cups skinned and boned
   chicken breast, cooked
225 g/8 oz mushrooms
2 garlic cloves, crushed
30 ml/2 tbsp chopped fresh parsley
15 ml/1 tbsp chopped fresh tarragon
1 egg, beaten
salt and pepper
fresh lemon juice
12–18 cannelloni tubes
1 recipe Napoletana Sauce
50 g/2 oz/½ cup freshly grated
   Parmesan cheese
1 sprig fresh parsley, to garnish

cannelloni tubes   *parsley*

garlic

egg

Parmesan cheese   *chicken*

1 Pre-heat the oven to 200°C/400°F/gas mark 6. Place the chicken in a food processor and blend until finely minced (ground). Transfer to a bowl.

2 Place the mushrooms, garlic, parsley and tarragon in the food processor and blend until finely minced.

3 Beat the mushroom mixture into the chicken with the egg, salt and pepper and lemon juice to taste.

4 If necessary, cook the cannelloni in plenty of salted boiling water according to the instructions. Drain well on a clean tea (dish) towel.

5 Place the filling in a piping bag (cone) fitted with a large plain nozzle (tip). Use this to fill each tube of cannelloni.

6 Lay the filled cannelloni tightly together in a single layer in a buttered shallow ovenproof dish. Spoon over the tomato sauce and sprinkle with Parmesan cheese. Bake in the oven for 30 minutes or until brown and bubbling. Serve garnished with a sprig of parsley.

Spaghetti alla Carbonara

It has been said that this dish was originally cooked by Italian coal miners or charcoal-burners, hence the name 'carbonara'. The secret of its creamy sauce is not to overcook the egg.

Serves 4

INGREDIENTS
175 g/6 oz unsmoked streaky bacon
1 garlic clove, chopped
3 eggs
450 g/1 lb spaghetti
salt and pepper
60 ml/4 tbsp freshly grated Parmesan
    cheese

bacon

garlic

eggs

spaghetti

Parmesan cheese

1 Cut the bacon into dice and place in a medium saucepan. Place over the heat and fry in its own fat with the garlic until brown. Keep warm until needed.

2 Whisk the eggs together in a bowl.

3 Cook the spaghetti in plenty of boiling salted water according to the manufacturer's instructions until *al dente*. Drain well.

4 Quickly turn the spaghetti into the pan with the bacon and stir in the eggs, a little salt, lots of pepper and half the cheese. Toss well to mix. The eggs should half-cook with the heat from the spaghetti. Serve in warm bowls with the remaining cheese.

Pasta with Bolognese Sauce

Traditional Bolognese sauce contains chicken livers to add richness, but you can leave them out and replace with an equal quantity of minced (ground) beef.

Serves 4–6

INGREDIENTS

75 g/3 oz pancetta or bacon in a piece
100 g/4 oz chicken livers
50 g/2 oz/4 tbsp butter, plus extra for tossing the pasta
1 medium onion, finely chopped
1 medium carrot, diced
1 celery stick, finely chopped
225 g/8 oz/2 cups lean minced (ground) beef
30 ml/2 tbsp tomato purée (paste)
100 ml/4 fl oz/½ cup white wine
200 ml/7 fl oz/1 cup beef stock or water
salt and pepper
freshly grated nutmeg
450 g/1 lb tagliatelle, spaghetti or fettuccine
freshly grated Parmesan cheese, to serve

tagliatelle

carrot

chicken livers

onion

celery

bacon

minced (ground) beef

1 Cut the pancetta into dice. Trim the chicken livers, removing any fat or gristle and any 'green' bits which will be bitter if left on. Roughly chop the livers.

2 Melt 50 g/2 oz/4 tbsp butter in a saucepan and add the bacon. Cook for 2–3 minutes until beginning to brown. Add the onion, carrot and celery and brown these too.

COOK'S TIP

If you like a richer sauce, stir in 150 ml/5 fl oz/⅔ cup double (heavy) cream or milk when the sauce has finished cooking.

3 Stir in the minced (ground) beef and brown over a high heat, breaking it up with a spoon. Stir in the chicken livers and cook for 2–3 minutes. Add the tomato purée (paste), mix well and pour in the wine and stock. Season well with salt, pepper and nutmeg. Bring to the boil, cover and simmer gently for about 35 minutes, stirring occasionally.

4 Cook the pasta in plenty of boiling salted water according to the manufacturer's instructions. Drain well and toss with the extra butter. Toss the meat sauce with the pasta and serve with plenty of Parmesan cheese.

Fettuccine all'Alfredo

A classic dish from Rome, Fettuccine all'Alfredo is simply pasta tossed with double (heavy) cream, butter and freshly grated Parmesan cheese. Popular additions are peas and strips of ham.

Serves 4

INGREDIENTS
25 g/1 oz/2 tbsp butter
150 ml/5 fl oz/²⁄₃ cup double (heavy)
    cream, plus 60 ml/4 tbsp extra
450 g/1 lb fettuccine
freshly grated nutmeg
salt and pepper
50 g/2 oz/½ cup freshly grated
    Parmesan cheese, plus extra to
    serve

fettuccine

nutmeg

Parmesan cheese

1 Place the butter and 150 ml/5 fl oz/²⁄₃ cup cream in a heavy saucepan, bring to the boil and simmer for 1 minute until slightly thickened.

2 Cook the fettuccine in plenty of boiling salted water according to the manufacturer's instructions, but for 2 minutes' less time. The pasta should still be a little firm.

3 Drain very well and turn into the pan with the cream sauce.

4 Place on the heat and turn the pasta in the sauce to coat.

5 Add the extra 60 ml/4 tbsp cream, the cheese, salt and pepper to taste and a little grated nutmeg. Toss until well coated and heated through. Serve immediately with extra grated Parmesan cheese.

Spaghetti Olio e Aglio

This is another classic recipe from Rome. A quick and filling dish, originally the food of the poor involving nothing more than pasta, garlic and olive oil, but now fast becoming fashionable.

Serves 4

INGREDIENTS
2 garlic cloves
30 ml/2 tbsp fresh parsley
100 ml/4 fl oz/½ cup olive oil
450 g/1 lb spaghetti
salt and pepper

spaghetti

olive oil

parsley

garlic

1 Finely chop the garlic.

2 Chop the parsley roughly.

3 Heat the olive oil in a medium saucepan and add the garlic and a pinch of salt. Cook gently, stirring all the time, until golden. If the garlic becomes too brown, it will taste bitter.

4 Meanwhile cook the spaghetti in plenty of boiling salted water according to the manufacturer's instructions until *al dente*. Drain well.

5 Toss with the warm – not sizzling – garlic and oil and add plenty of black pepper and the parsley. Serve immediately.

Paglia e Fieno

The title of this dish translates as 'straw and hay' which refers to the yellow and green colours of the pasta when mixed together. Using fresh peas makes all the difference to this dish.

Serves 4

INGREDIENTS
50 g/2 oz/4 tbsp butter
350 g/12 oz/2 cups frozen petits pois (small peas) or 900 g/2 lb fresh peas, shelled
150 ml/5 fl oz/⅔ cup double (heavy) cream, plus 60 ml/4 tbsp extra
450 g/1 lb tagliatelle (plain and spinach mixed)
50 g/2 oz/½ cup freshly grated Parmesan cheese, plus extra to serve
salt and pepper
freshly grated nutmeg

tagliatelle

peas

Parmesan cheese

COOK'S TIP

Sautéed mushrooms and narrow strips of cooked ham also make a good addition.

1 Melt the butter in a heavy saucepan and add the peas. Sauté for 2–3 minutes, then add the cream, bring to the boil and simmer for 1 minute until slightly thickened.

2 Cook the fettuccine in plenty of boiling salted water according to the manufacturer's instructions, but for 2 minutes' less time. The pasta should still be *al dente*. Drain very well and turn into the pan with the cream and pea sauce.

3 Place on the heat and turn the pasta in the sauce to coat. Pour in the extra cream, the cheese, salt and pepper to taste and a little grated nutmeg. Toss until well coated and heated through. Serve immediately with extra Parmesan cheese.

Pasta Napoletana

The simple classic cooked tomato sauce with no adornments.

Serves 4

INGREDIENTS

900 g/2 lb fresh ripe red tomatoes or
  800 g/1¾ lb canned plum tomatoes
  with juice
1 medium onion, chopped
1 medium carrot, diced
1 celery stick, diced
150 ml/5 fl oz/⅔ cup dry white wine
  (optional)
1 sprig fresh parsley
salt and pepper
pinch of caster (superfine) sugar
15 ml/1 tbsp chopped fresh oregano
  or 5 ml/1 tsp dried oregano
450 g/1 lb/4 cups pasta, any variety
freshly grated Parmesan cheese, to
  serve

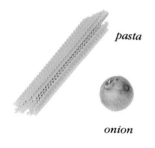

pasta

onion

tomatoes

celery

parsley

carrot

Parmesan cheese

1 Roughly chop the tomatoes and place in a medium saucepan.

2 Put all the ingredients except the oregano, pasta and cheese into the pan containing the tomatoes, bring to the boil and simmer, half-covered, for 45 minutes until very thick, stirring occasionally. Pass through a sieve (strainer) or liquidize and sieve (strain) to remove the tomato seeds, then stir in the oregano. Taste to check the seasoning.

3 Cook the pasta in plenty of boiling salted water according to the manufacturer's instructions until *al dente*. Drain well.

4 Toss the pasta with the sauce. Serve with grated Parmesan cheese.

Pasta with Pesto Sauce

Don't stint on the fresh basil – this is the most wonderful sauce in the world! There are now good fresh pesto sauces in the chilled cabinets of large supermarkets. They taste completely different from the pesto sold in jars.

Serves 4

INGREDIENTS
2 garlic cloves
salt and pepper
50 g/2 oz/½ cup pine nuts
50 g/2 oz/1 cup fresh basil leaves
150 ml/5 fl oz/⅔ cup olive oil (not extra-virgin as it is too strong)
50 g/2 oz/4 tbsp unsalted butter, softened
60 ml/4 tbsp freshly grated Parmesan cheese
450 g/1 lb spaghetti

olive oil

spaghetti

pine nuts

Parmesan cheese

basil

1 Peel the garlic and process in a food processor with a little salt and the pine nuts until broken up. Add the basil leaves and continue mixing to a paste.

2 Gradually add the olive oil, little by little, until the mixture is creamy and thick.

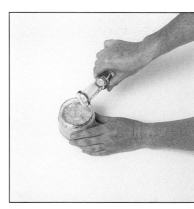

3 Beat in the butter and season with pepper. Beat in the cheese. (Alternatively, you can make the pesto by hand using a pestle and mortar.)

4 Store the pesto in a jar (with a layer of olive oil on top to exclude the air) in the fridge until needed.

5 Cook the pasta in plenty of boiling salted water according to the manufacturer's instructions. Drain well.

COOK'S TIP

A good pesto can be made using parsley instead of basil and walnuts instead of pine nuts. To make it go further, add a spoonful or two of fromage frais. 'Red' pesto includes sun-dried tomato paste and pounded roasted red peppers.

6 Toss the pasta with half the pesto and serve in warm bowls with the remaining pesto spooned on top.

Rotolo di Pasta

A giant Swiss (jelly) roll of pasta with a spinach filling, which is poached, sliced and baked with béchamel or tomato sauce. Use fresh home-made pasta for this recipe, or ask your local Italian deli to make a large sheet of pasta for you!

Serves 6

INGREDIENTS
700 g/1½ lb frozen chopped spinach, thawed
50 g/2 oz/4 tbsp butter
1 medium onion, chopped
100 g/4 oz ham or bacon, diced
225 g/8 oz ricotta or curd (cottage) cheese
1 egg
salt and pepper
freshly grated nutmeg
fresh spinach pasta made with 2 eggs and 200 g/7 oz/1¾ cups flour
1.25 litres/2¼ pints/5½ cups Béchamel Sauce, warmed
50 g/2 oz/½ cup freshly grated Parmesan cheese

onion

ricotta cheese

spinach

nutmeg

ham

1 Squeeze the excess moisture from the spinach and set aside.

2 Melt the butter in a saucepan and fry the onion until golden. Add the ham and fry until beginning to brown. Take off the heat and stir in the spinach. Cool slightly, then beat in the ricotta and egg. Season well with salt, pepper and nutmeg.

3 Roll the pasta out to a rectangle about 30 × 40 cm/12 × 16 in. Spread the filling all over, leaving a 1 cm/½ in border all round the edge.

4 Roll up from the shorter end and wrap in muslin (cheesecloth) to form a 'sausage', tying the ends securely with string. Poach in a very large pan (or fish kettle) of simmering water for 20 minutes or until firm. Carefully remove, drain and unwrap. Cool.

5 When you are ready to finish the dish, pre-heat the oven to 200°C/400°F/ gas mark 6. Cut the pasta roll into 2.5 cm/ 1 in slices. Spoon a little béchamel sauce over the base of a shallow baking dish and arrange the slices slightly overlapping each other.

6 Spoon over the remaining sauce, sprinkle with the cheese and bake in the oven for 15–20 minutes or until browned and bubbling. Allow to stand for a few minutes before serving.

Pasta, Melon and Prawn Salad

Orange-fleshed cantaloupe or Charentais melon looks spectacular in this salad. You could also use a mixture of ogen, cantaloupe and water melon.

Serves 4–6

INGREDIENTS
175 g/6 oz/1½ cups pasta shapes
225 g/8 oz frozen prawns (shrimp),
    thawed and drained
1 large or 2 small melons
60 ml/4 tbsp olive oil
15 ml/1 tbsp tarragon vinegar
30 ml/2 tbsp chopped fresh chives or
    parsley
sprigs of herbs, to garnish
shredded Chinese leaves, to serve

melons

pasta shapes

prawns (shrimp)

Chinese leaves

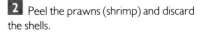

1 Cook the pasta in boiling salted water according to the manufacturer's instructions. Drain well and allow to cool.

2 Peel the prawns (shrimp) and discard the shells.

3 Halve the melon and remove the seeds with a teaspoon. Carefully scoop the flesh into balls with a melon baller and mix with the prawns and pasta.

4 Whisk the oil, vinegar and chopped herbs together. Pour on to the prawn mixture and turn to coat. Cover and chill for at least 30 minutes.

5 Meanwhile shred the Chinese leaves and use to line a shallow bowl or the empty melon halves.

6 Pile the prawn mixture on to the Chinese leaves and garnish with herbs.

Avocado, Tomato and Mozzarella Pasta Salad with Pine Nuts

A salad made from ingredients representing the colours of the Italian flag – a sunny cheerful dish!

Serves 4

INGREDIENTS
175 g/6 oz/1½ cups pasta bows
    (farfalle)
6 ripe red tomatoes
225 g/8 oz mozzarella cheese
1 large ripe avocado
30 ml/2 tbsp pine nuts, toasted
1 sprig fresh basil, to garnish

DRESSING
90 ml/6 tbsp olive oil
30 ml/2 tbsp wine vinegar
5 ml/1 tsp balsamic vinegar (optional)
5 ml/1 tsp wholegrain mustard
pinch of sugar
salt and pepper
30 ml/2 tbsp chopped fresh basil

olive oil

avocado

tomatoes

basil

mozzarella cheese

pine nuts   *pasta bows*

1 Cook the pasta in plenty of boiling salted water according to the manufacturer's instructions. Drain well and cool.

2 Slice the tomatoes and mozzarella cheese into thin rounds.

3 Halve the avocado, remove the stone (pit) and peel off the skin. Slice the flesh lengthways.

4 Whisk all the dressing ingredients together in a small bowl.

5 Arrange the tomato, mozzarella and avocado in overlapping slices around the edge of a flat plate.

6 Toss the pasta with half the dressing and the chopped basil. Pile into the centre of the plate. Pour over the remaining dressing, scatter over the pine nuts and garnish with a sprig of fresh basil. Serve immediately.

Wholemeal Pasta, Asparagus and Potato Salad with Parmesan

A meal in itself, this is a real treat when made with fresh asparagus just in season.

Serves 4

INGREDIENTS
225 g/8 oz/2 cups wholemeal (whole-wheat) pasta shapes
60 ml/4 tbsp extra-virgin olive oil
salt and pepper
350 g/12 oz baby new potatoes
225 g/8 oz fresh asparagus
100 g/4 oz piece fresh Parmesan cheese

olive oil

asparagus

Parmesan cheese

pasta shapes

new potatoes

1 Cook the pasta in boiling salted water according to the manufacturer's instructions. Drain well and toss with the olive oil, salt and pepper while still warm.

2 Wash the potatoes and cook in boiling salted water for 12–15 minutes or until tender. Drain and toss with the pasta.

3 Trim any woody ends off the asparagus and halve the stalks if very long. Blanch in boiling salted water for 6 minutes until bright green and still crunchy. Drain. Plunge into cold water to stop them cooking and allow to cool. Drain and dry on kitchen paper.

4 Toss the asparagus with the potatoes and pasta, season and transfer to a shallow bowl. Using a rotary vegetable peeler, shave the Parmesan over the salad.

Roquefort and Walnut Pasta Salad

This is a simple earthy salad, relying totally on the quality of the ingredients. There is no real substitute for the Roquefort — a blue-veined ewe's-milk cheese from south-western France.

Serves 4

INGREDIENTS

225 g/8 oz/2 cups pasta shapes
selection of salad leaves (such as
    rocket (arugula), curly endive,
    lamb's lettuce, baby spinach,
    radicchio, etc.)
30 ml/2 tbsp walnut oil
60 ml/4 tbsp sunflower oil
30 ml/2 tbsp red wine vinegar or
    sherry vinegar
salt and pepper
225 g/8 oz Roquefort cheese, roughly
    crumbled
100 g/4 oz/1 cup walnut halves

pasta shapes

Roquefort cheese   *walnuts*

salad leaves

1 Cook the pasta in plenty of boiling salted water according to the manufacturer's instructions. Drain well and cool. Wash and dry the salad leaves and place in a bowl.

2 Whisk together the walnut oil, sunflower oil, vinegar and salt and pepper to taste.

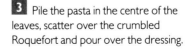

3 Pile the pasta in the centre of the leaves, scatter over the crumbled Roquefort and pour over the dressing.

4 Scatter over the walnuts. Toss just before serving.

COOK'S TIP

Try toasting the walnuts under the grill (broiler) for a couple of minutes to release the flavour.

Mediterranean Salad with Basil

A type of Salade Niçoise with pasta, conjuring up all the sunny flavours of the Mediterranean.

Serves 4

INGREDIENTS
225 g/8 oz/2 cups chunky pasta shapes
175 g/6 oz fine green beans
2 large ripe tomatoes
50 g/2 oz fresh basil leaves
200 g/7 oz can tuna fish in oil, drained
2 hard-boiled eggs, shelled and sliced
   or quartered
50 g/2 oz can anchovy fillets, drained
capers and black olives

DRESSING
90 ml/6 tbsp extra-virgin olive oil
30 ml/2 tbsp white wine vinegar or
   lemon juice
2 garlic cloves, crushed
2.5 ml/½ tsp Dijon mustard
30 ml/2 tbsp chopped fresh basil
salt and pepper

tomatoes

olive oil

garlic

basil

pasta shapes

egg

anchovy fillets

green beans

tuna fish

1 Whisk all the ingredients for the dressing together and leave to infuse while you make the salad.

2 Cook the pasta in plenty of boiling salted water according to the manufacturer's instructions. Drain well and cool.

3 Trim the beans and blanch in boiling salted water for 3 minutes. Drain and refresh in cold water.

4 Slice or quarter the tomatoes and arrange on the bottom of a bowl. Moisten with a little dressing and cover with a quarter of the basil leaves. Then cover with the beans. Moisten with a little more dressing and cover with a third of the remaining basil.

5 Cover with the pasta tossed in a little more dressing, half the remaining basil and the roughly flaked tuna.

6 Arrange the eggs on top, then finally scatter over the anchovy fillets, capers and black olives. Pour over the remaining dressing and garnish with the remaining basil. Serve immediately. Don't be tempted to chill this salad – all the flavour will be dulled.

Dark Chocolate Ravioli with White Chocolate and Cream Cheese Filling

This is a spectacular, chocolatey pasta, with cocoa powder added to the flour. The pasta packets contain a rich creamy-white filling.

Serves 4

INGREDIENTS
175 g/6 oz/1½ cups plain white (all-purpose) flour
25 g/1 oz/¼ cup cocoa powder
30 ml/2 tbsp icing (confectioner's) sugar
2 large eggs
salt
single (light) cream and grated chocolate, to serve

FILLING
175 g/6 oz white chocolate
350 g/12 oz/3 cups cream cheese
1 egg, plus 1 beaten egg to seal

cream cheese

eggs

cocoa powder

white chocolate

1 Make the pasta following the instructions for Basic Pasta Dough, but sifting the flour with the cocoa and icing sugar before adding the eggs. Cover and rest for at least 30 minutes.

2 For the filling, break up the white chocolate and melt it in a basin standing in a pan of barely simmering water. Cool slightly, then beat into the cream cheese with the egg. Spoon into a piping bag (cone) fitted with a plain nozzle (tip).

3 Cut the dough in half and wrap one portion in clear film (plastic wrap). Roll the pasta out thinly to a rectangle on a lightly floured surface, or use a pasta machine. Cover with a clean damp tea (dish) towel and repeat with the remaining pasta.

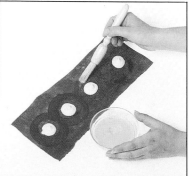

4 Pipe small mounds (about 5 ml/1 tsp) of filling in even rows, spacing them at 4 cm/1½ in intervals, across one piece of the dough. Using a pastry brush, brush the spaces of dough between the mounds with beaten egg.

5 Using a rolling pin, lift the remaining sheet of pasta over the dough with the filling. Press down firmly between the pockets of filling, pushing out any trapped air. Cut into rounds with a serrated ravioli cutter or sharp knife. Transfer to a floured tea (dish) towel. Rest for 1 hour.

6 Bring a large pan of salted water to the boil and add the ravioli a few at a time, stirring to prevent them sticking together. Simmer gently for 3–5 minutes, remove with a perforated spoon and serve with a generous splash of single (light) cream and grated chocolate.

Crisp Vermicelli Cakes with Honey and Walnuts

In this recipe the pasta is double-cooked for crispness, then soaked in honey and nuts to give a Middle Eastern flavour.

Serves 4

INGREDIENTS

225 g/8 oz/2 cups vermicelli or angel
   hair pasta
salt
100 g/4 oz/½ cup butter
175 g/6 oz/1½ cups mixed nuts, such
   as walnuts and pistachios
100 g/4 oz/½ cup granulated sugar
100 g/4 oz/⅓ cup clear honey
10 ml/2 tsp lemon juice

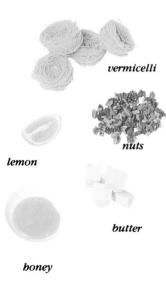

vermicelli

nuts

lemon

butter

honey

1 Pre-heat the oven to 180°C/350°F/ gas mark 4. Cook the pasta in pienty of boiling salted water according to the manufacturer's instructions. Drain well, return to the pan with the butter and toss in the residual heat to coat. Cool.

2 Set 4 crumpet (poaching) rings on baking sheets. Divide the pasta into 8 mounds, then lightly press a mound of pasta evenly into each ring.

3 Chop the nuts and sprinkle half over the pasta. Top each ring with a mound of the remaining pasta and press down well. Bake in the oven for 40–45 minutes or until golden-brown.

4 Meanwhile place the sugar, honey and 150 ml/5 fl oz/⅔ cup water in a medium saucepan and slowly bring to the boil, making sure that all the sugar is dissolved before it boils. Simmer for 10 minutes, add the lemon juice and simmer for a further 5 minutes. Set aside.

5 Carefully remove the baked pasta from the rings and place in an even layer on a shallow dish.

6 Pour over the syrup and scatter with the remaining nuts. Cool completely before serving.

Cinnamon Tagliatelle with Creamy Custard Sauce

The secret of this pudding is to roll the pasta out very thinly, giving delicious ribbons coated in a delicate vanilla sauce.

Serves 4

INGREDIENTS
175 g/6 oz/1½ cups plain white (all-purpose) flour
pinch of salt
30 ml/2 tbsp icing (confectioner's) sugar
10 ml/2 tsp ground cinnamon, plus extra for dusting the pasta
2 large eggs
melted butter, for tossing the pasta

CUSTARD
1 vanilla pod (bean)
600 ml/1 pint/2½ cups milk
6 egg yolks
50–75 g/2–3 oz/¼–⅓ cup caster (superfine) sugar

eggs

butter

cinnamon

vanilla pod (bean)

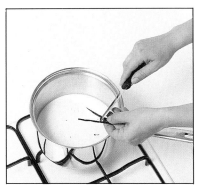

1 Make the pasta following the instructions for Basic Pasta Dough, but sifting the flour with the icing (confectioner's) sugar and cinnamon before adding the eggs. Roll out thinly and cut into tagliatelle. Spread out on a clean, lightly floured tea (dish) towel to dry.

2 For the custard, split the vanilla pod (bean) and scrape out the seeds into a saucepan. Add the pod itself to the pan with the milk and slowly bring to the boil. Take the pan off the heat and allow to infuse for 10 minutes, then strain to remove the vanilla pod and seeds.

3 Whisk the egg yolks and sugar together in a medium bowl until pale and creamy. Slowly stir in the strained milk, return the pan to a low heat and cook, stirring, until slightly thickened. Do not boil or the custard will curdle. Strain and keep warm.

4 Drop the tagliatelle into plenty of boiling salted water and cook until the water returns to the boil or until al dente. The pasta should have no hard core, and should be very pliable. Strain and toss with a little butter. Serve in warm bowls with the custard poured over. Dust with extra cinnamon if liked.

Tiramisu Surprise

The small pasta shapes incorporated into this dessert make a very pretty dish served in tall glasses.

Serves 4

INGREDIENTS
100 g/4 oz/1 cup small pasta shapes
salt
16 small ratafias, macaroons or
    Amaretti biscuits (cookies)
90 ml/6 tbsp very strong black coffee
30 ml/2 tbsp brandy
60 ml/4 tbsp dark rum
400 g/14 oz/1¾ cups mascarpone or
    other cream cheese
50 g/2 oz/½ cup icing
    (confectioner's) sugar, sifted
150 ml/5 fl oz/⅔ cup whipping cream
75 g/3 oz chocolate shavings, to
    decorate

dark rum

pasta shapes

brandy *chocolate*

ratafias

1 Cook the pasta in plenty of boiling salted water according to the manufacturer's instructions. Drain well and cool.

2 Place the ratafias in 4 individual glasses and spoon over a layer of pasta. Mix together the coffee, brandy and 30 ml/2 tbsp of the rum and pour this over the pasta layer.

3 Beat the mascarpone with the sugar and remaining rum until smooth. Stir in the cream and spoon the mixture equally between the glasses.

4 Sprinkle the chocolate shavings thickly on top of the cheese mixture to decorate and refrigerate for at least 1 hour before serving.

Pasta Timbales with Apricot Sauce

Orzo or rice-shaped pasta inspired this dessert made like a rice pudding, but with a difference! Other small soup pastas can be used if orzo cannot be found.

Serves 4

INGREDIENTS

100 g/4 oz/1 cup orzo or other soup
    pasta
75 g/3 oz/¹⁄₃ cup caster (superfine)
    sugar
salt
25 g/1 oz/2 tbsp butter
1 vanilla pod (bean), split
750 ml/1¼ pints/3²⁄₃ cups milk
300 ml/10 fl oz/1¼ cups ready-made
    custard
45 ml/3 tbsp kirsch
15 ml/1 tbsp powdered gelatine
oil, for greasing
400 g/14 oz canned apricots in juice
lemon juice
fresh flowers, to decorate (optional)

custard

butter

pasta

apricots

lemon

1 Place the pasta, sugar, a pinch of salt, the butter, vanilla pod (bean) and milk into a heavy saucepan and bring to the boil. Turn down the heat and simmer for 25 minutes until the pasta is tender and most of the liquid is absorbed. Stir frequently to prevent it from sticking.

2 Remove the vanilla pod and transfer the pasta to a bowl to cool. Stir in the custard and 30 ml/2 tbsp of the kirsch.

3 Sprinkle the gelatine over 45 ml/ 2 tbsp water in a small bowl set in a pan of barely simmering water. Allow to become spongy and heat gently to dissolve. Stir into the pasta.

4 Lightly oil 4 timbale moulds and spoon in the pasta. Refrigerate for 2 hours until set.

5 Meanwhile liquidize the apricots, pass through a sieve (strainer) and add lemon juice and kirsch to taste. Dilute with a little water if too thick.

6 Loosen the pasta timbales from their moulds and turn out on to individual plates. Spoon some apricot sauce around and serve, decorated with a few fresh flowers if liked.

Strawberry Conchiglie Salad with Kirsch and Raspberry Sauce

A divinely decadent dessert laced with liqueur and luscious raspberry sauce.

Serves 4

INGREDIENTS
175 g/6 oz/½ cup pasta shells (conchiglie)
salt
225 g/8 oz fresh or frozen raspberries, thawed if frozen
15–30 ml/1–2 tbsp caster (superfine) sugar
lemon juice
450 g/1 lb small fresh strawberries
flaked almonds
45 ml/3 tbsp kirsch

pasta shells

raspberries

strawberries

almonds

1 Cook the pasta in plenty of boiling salted water according to the manufacturer's instructions. Drain well and cool.

2 Purée the raspberries in a food processor and pass through a sieve (strainer) to remove the seeds.

3 Put the purée in a small saucepan with the sugar and simmer for 5–6 minutes, stirring occasionally. Add lemon juice to taste. Set aside to cool.

4 Hull the strawberries and halve if necessary. Toss with the pasta and transfer to a serving bowl.

5 Spread the almonds on a baking sheet and toast under the grill (broiler) until golden. Cool.

6 Stir the kirsch into the raspberry sauce and pour over the salad. Scatter with the toasted almonds and serve.

INDEX